PULLING MY LEG

story by **JO CARSON**
pictures by **JULIE DOWNING**

ORCHARD BOOKS   NEW YORK

Orchard Books, A division of Franklin Watts, Inc., 387 Park Avenue South, New York, NY 10016

Manufactured in the United States of America. Printed by General Offset Company, Inc.
Bound by Horowitz / Rae. Book design by Mina Greenstein.
The text of this book is set in 16 pt. Gamma Book. The illustrations are color pencil.

2   4   6   8   10   9   7   5   3   1

Library of Congress Cataloging-in-Publication Data
Carson, Jo.   Pulling my leg / by Jo Carson ; illustrated by Julie Downing.   p.   cm.   "A Richard Jack-
son book."   Summary: When a joking uncle collects hammer, pliers, and screwdriver to help a child
with her loose tooth, the tooth amazingly comes out by itself.   ISBN 0-531-05817-4.
ISBN 0-531-08417-5 (lib. bdg.)   [1. Teeth—Fiction.   2. Uncles—Fiction.]   I. Downing, Julie, ill.
II. Title.   PZ7.C2625Pu   1990   [E]—dc20   89-70978   CIP   AC

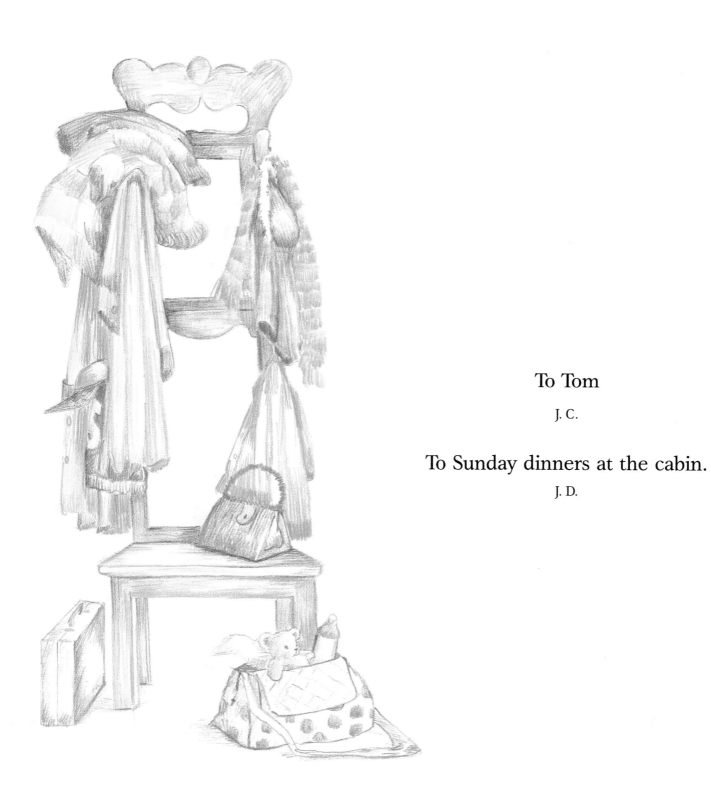

To Tom

J. C.

To Sunday dinners at the cabin.

J. D.

I had a loose tooth. It wobbled.
I pushed it around with my tongue
all during Grandma's birthday dinner.
"I can't eat with a tooth this loose," I said.
We were having pork chops.

"Poor child could waste away," said Uncle Tom.
"It's time for an ex-trac-tion!"

"What's that?"

"I'll show you. First you'll have to get
a pair of pliers."

I found pliers in Grandpa's tackle box
(with the hooks and spinners and sinkers and line
that sank deeper than I could see when we went fishing)
and I carried the pliers back to Uncle Tom.

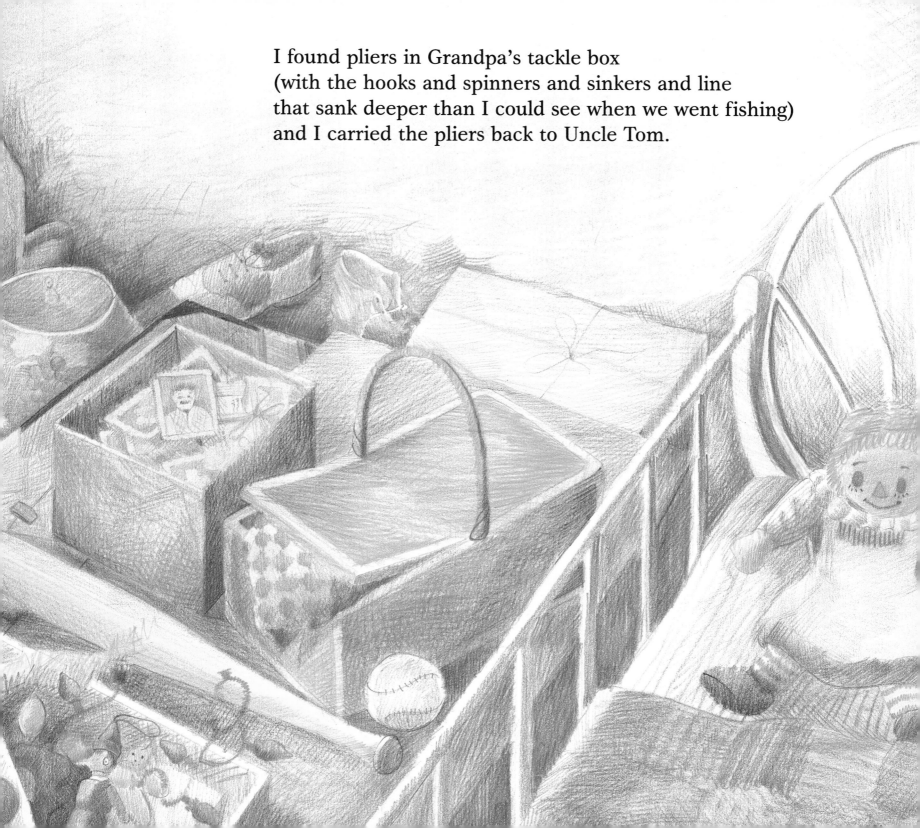

I opened my mouth and Tom looked in.
"Oh," he said, "it's worse than I imagined.
  I'll need a hammer."

"A hammer?"

"I'm going to have to bust this old tooth loose."

"It's already loose!" I poked it with my tongue.

"Who can see it," asked Tom, "me or you? It might turn out
  that we don't need a hammer, but we should have it
  just in case."

I found the hammer in Grandma's kitchen drawers
(with the knives and sieves and measures and spoons with holes
she used when she made chocolate icing),
and I carried the hammer back to Uncle Tom.

I opened up my mouth again and Tom looked in.
"I'm afraid I have to have a screwdriver," he said.

"There aren't any screws in my mouth!" I said. "I can pull this tooth
any time I want."

"That's what you think. I'm going to have to pry it out. You want to hunt a screwdriver or a crowbar?"

I found a screwdriver in the garage.
(I looked for the blacksnake, Shakespeare,
but he wasn't in his usual place.)

Grandpa's dog, Hoover, lay in the sun
and wagged his tail when I spoke.
"It's hard to know whether Uncle Tom
is pulling my leg or my tooth," I told him.

The tooth was very loose. I poked it with my tongue
some more and carried the screwdriver in to Uncle Tom.

"You don't really need this," I said.

"We'll see," said Tom. "Now, open wide." He had the hammer
  in one hand, the pliers and screwdriver in the other.
"I'm going to knock it first and then I'm going to twist it
  and then I'm going to pry it out."

"I think I want
to wait a minute."

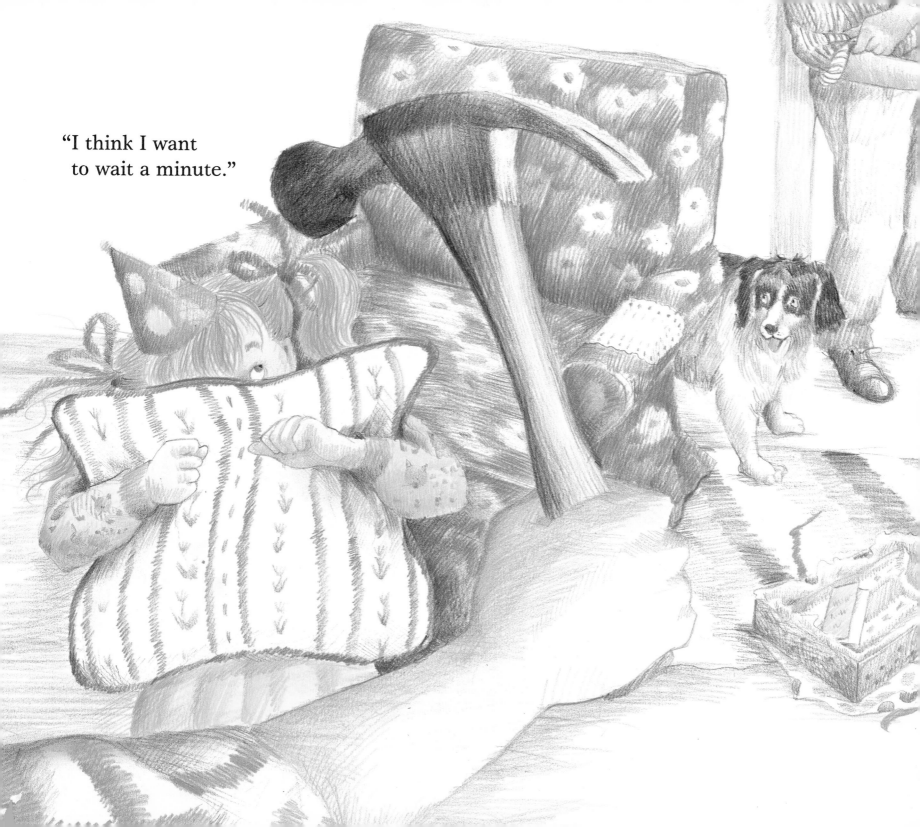

"Oh," said Uncle Tom, "she's getting scared. Nothing harder than pulling chickens' teeth!"

He called my father to hold me down. "Don't let her wiggle, it makes it worse."

"I can eat some mashed potatoes," I said.

"And don't tickle her," said Tom,
   but my daddy was already doing that.
"And get her feet and tie her arms....
   I have to see my way clear
   to her mouth!"

"STOP!"
And I took the tooth out of my mouth. "Came loose."
I showed it right up close to Uncle Tom.

"I guess it wasn't wedged in as bad as it looked," said Tom.

"Guess not," I said.

I put the tooth in my pocket.

And then Tom said, "I hear the tooth fairy has gone up
to fifty cents, but I'll give you a quarter here and now.
I'll put that tooth under my pillow and let you know what happens…."

"Tooth fairy won't pay you," I said. "It's not your tooth."

"…And one more thing," said Tom. "If you don't put your tongue in the tooth hole, that tooth will grow back solid gold."

"You're just pulling my leg."

"We can do that if you want to," Tom began,
"but you'll have to find about
twenty feet of rope...."